BACK & FORTH

A Family Resource

1 2 3 4 5 6 7 8 9 0 1 2 3 4 5 6 7 8 9

Back and Forth: A Family Resource
By Debbie Trafton O'Neal

Augsburg Fortress, Minneapolis

Living in Grace Confirmation Series

Editors: Sonia A. Albers and Virginia Bonde Zarth
Series Designer: Evans McCormick Creative

Scripture quotations are from New Revised Standard Version Bible, copyright 1989 Division of Christian Education of the National Council of the Churches of Christ in the United States of America. Used by permission.

Catechism quotations are from A Contemporary Translation of Luther's Small Catechism: Study Edition, copyright © 1994 Augsburg Fortress.

ISBN 0-8066-0229-5

Manufactured in U.S.A.

Faith Have you ever been in a noisy crowd of people rushing to and fro? Maybe the first Pentecost was like that. But God spoke to and through the people there. They just needed to listen to what God was saying to them.

Live it! In our busy world, it can be difficult to sit still and be quiet long enough to listen to the Holy Spirit. One way to do this is to talk with your family and the people close to you about God in your life. As you do this, the Holy Spirit will guide all that you say and do.

FAITH "Now I lay me down to sleep . . ." Is this the first prayer you learned? Do you still know the first prayer you learned? What is it?

LIVE IT! Write a family prayer to unite your family. How about a prayer to begin the day, a grace to say before a meal, or a prayer to end the day when everyone is home safely?

1
PRAYER

Faith Imagine the joy of the women who first discovered that Jesus' tomb was empty on Easter morning. Sometimes in the quiet hush of dawn, we can spend a moment in that garden.

Live it!

Where is your special place? Everyone needs one—a place to go when you need a moment to remind yourself of who you are and whose you are. If you don't have a place like this, find one.

Faith God answers prayer! Talk with your family about some of the prayers God has answered. Does God always answer prayers the way you would like?

Live it! Keep a jar of prayers. Every time God answers a prayer (even if it's not the answer you hoped for), put a marble or penny in a second jar to remind you that God answers prayers.

Faith Jesus said we should love our neighbor as we love ourselves (see Luke 10:27). Sometimes this isn't easy to do! Think back to when someone loved you at a time when you were not very lovable.

Live it! How can you and your family be good neighbors? Don't just talk about it—take action! Be God's hands in your world today.

Faith There is a prayer that says, "The sea is so big and my boat is so small." It is easy to feel that our little prayers won't make a difference in a world full of problems. But they do.

Live it! How can your family use the news to prompt your prayers? You can pray for people in the headlines or pray for the reporters and photographers.

3
PRAYER

FAITH The New Testament is full of words that tell us about new life. Jesus made many comparisons to new life being like things around us. (Read a few of them in Luke 15.) What are symbols of new life to you?

NEW TESTAMENT

LIVE IT! As a family, plant a tree or other plant as a symbol of your new life in Christ. A plant needs nourishment and care for healthy growth, just like people do. Don't neglect it!

FAITH Martin Luther said it was good to make the sign of the cross as soon as you get out of bed in the morning. Have you ever thought about starting your day this way?

LIVE IT! Make the sign of the cross, going from your forehead, to chest, to left shoulder, to right shoulder, every morning for a week. Dedicate your day and all that you do to God, asking for God's guidance and protection.

4
PRAYER

Faith Jesus told Peter he was the rock upon which the church would be built. Sometimes we say people are as solid as a rock, meaning that we can always count on them to be honest and trustworthy. Who is your rock?

Live it! Lots of people collect rocks. Ask everyone in your family to collect different kinds of rocks for a week and notice the variety. Keep your rock pile as a reminder of the church, built upon a rock.

Faith Do you ever sit at the breakfast table, crunching your cereal and slurping your juice in rhythm with the radio? Have you noticed that many times what you put into your head is what will come out of your mouth later that day?

Live it! Surprise someone in your family! Write the words to a morning prayer or to a favorite hymn on a piece of paper and tape it to a cereal box. Leave the cereal box on the table.

5

PRAYER

FAITH Christmas is a festive time for most families. What's best about it for you? Perhaps it's the awesome feeling that God gave us the greatest gift of all—his Son, Jesus.

LIVE IT! It's fun to shop for, wrap, and receive gifts. But some people don't ever experience this. Select someone to whom you do not usually give a gift and shop for a gift for them. Make their Christmas special.

Faith Little children (and sometimes bigger children) are often afraid of the dark. Leaving a light on in the hall can help. So can a prayer that asks for God's protection during the night.

Live it! Before you go to bed, make the sign of the cross and say, "Under the care of God the Father, Son, and Holy Spirit. Amen." Ask God for a restful night, in Jesus' name.

6
PRAYER

Faith It's amazing to stop and think about how many years the words in the Bible have been printed and read. What's even more amazing is to think about how many years these words have been shared among generations of believers by the telling and retelling of stories!

Live it! Family stories are fun to tell. Have you ever asked your parents to tell you about some of their funny times growing up?

Try it—you may be surprised how much you enjoy it.

FAITH Sometimes we take for granted all the good gifts God gives us—family, friends, a home, food, water, pets, clothing, and the list goes on. When do you stop to think about the ways God has blessed you?

LIVE IT! Tithing is a biblical concept that directs us to give 10 percent of what we have to God. Next time you shop for groceries, shop intentionally. Designate one of every 10 items you buy to give to a local food shelf.

FAITH "As for me and my household, we will serve the Lord" (Joshua 24:15). What do these words mean to you when you read them?

LIVE IT! Sometimes people have these words from Joshua over the doorway to their home. Talk with your family about how you as a family serve the Lord.

Faith The world would be an incredibly boring place if everyone were exactly the same. Isn't it great that God created people of all sizes, shapes, and colors?

Live it! Take your family on a people scavenger hunt in a local shopping center. Find people who are the same, and different, to appreciate the variety of people God gives us to enjoy.

8
OUR LIFE TOGETHER

Faith In the Old Testament there are many accounts of God speaking directly to people. Think of Abraham and Sarah, Jacob, and Moses. God is always ready to communicate with us. We just need to be listening.

Live it! We probably don't have the privilege of hearing God's voice booming out of the clouds or from a burning bush, but God may speak to us in quiet ways through other people and events in our lives. Pray a prayer that God will open your heart and mind to hear God's plan for you.

Faith Martin Luther felt that the power of the death and resurrection of Jesus Christ means that we do not have to escape the world by living only among "religious" people. Instead, we serve Christ and our neighbor in our daily life.

Live it! How do you and your family give evidence of your faith in your daily lives? Find these Bible verses to see what the Bible says about this: Ephesians 6:1-4, 1 John 3:16, 1 John 4:7, 1 Peter 5:5.

9
OUR LIFE TOGETHER

Faith Brothers and sisters! Sometimes they can be our greatest trial, no matter what age we are. Certainly Joseph must have thought that at some time after his brothers sold him; but Joseph trusted God, forgave his brothers, and lived a faith-filled life.

Live it! When was the last time you had an argument with your brother or sister or another family member? How did you resolve it? Pick a time when you're getting along and talk about the way you'd like to resolve your conflicts the next time they occur.

FAITH There are many people from whom we can learn. In the Bible, older people often taught their trades and talents to younger people, so that the knowledge would not be lost. Is there someone who could share his or her knowledge with you?

LIVE IT! A mentor is someone who is a trusted counselor or guide. Has someone in your church been a mentor to you? Can you think of someone to whom you can be a mentor? When you share your faith, it becomes more real to you.

OUR LIFE TOGETHER

FAITH There are lots of songs about Noah building the ark and taking the animals on board. The people around Noah must have thought he was crazy to build such a big boat! But Noah trusted God.

LIVE IT! Sometimes your day will take twists and turns you didn't plan on. It can be frustrating or it can be a time to trust God. Which will you choose?

Faith Does God want you to have fun? YES!!! Sometimes we forget this and don't make fun a part of our everyday life. What would you like to do with your family just for fun?

Live it! Have everyone in your family write ideas on slips of paper of what you could do for fun together. Fold them and put them in a box. At least once a week, pull out one of the slips of paper and have fun doing what it says!

OUR LIFE TOGETHER

Faith Do you remember the story of Samuel? (See 1 Samuel 1–3.) When God called Samuel, he answered, "Here I am, Lord." Have you heard God calling to you in some way? How did you respond?

Live it!

Think about all the ways you communicate: speaking, writing, telephoning, and perhaps by computer. How do you communicate with God? Remember, communication means talking *and listening*. Have a conversation with your family and think about how well you listen.

Faith It's been said, "A family that plays together, stays together." With our busy lives, it may be easy to put off spending time with our families and friends.

Live it! Get together with your family or with other families and plan a family fun night or a Saturday event at your church. Invite people to bring their favorite games, snacks, and musical instruments. This may be so much fun that it becomes a monthly event!

12
OUR LIFE TOGETHER

FAITH There is an old poem that reads something like this: "You are writing a gospel, a chapter each day, by the things that you do and the things that you say." Have you ever thought about life this way?

LIVE IT! There is an art to living your faith. How do you live out your faith? Share with each other what a chapter of your faith gospel may be.

Faith Rules aren't always fun. But have you ever played a game where there aren't any rules? That isn't much fun either! God must have known that when God gave the Ten Commandments to Moses.

Live it! Does your family have rules? Most families do, but often they're simply understood and not spelled out. Plan a time when everyone in your family can talk about the written and unwritten rules you have and why they are important. Write a family covenant that everyone signs.

13
TEN COMMANDMENTS

Faith During a storm on the water, Jesus admonished the disciples by referring to them as "you of little faith" (Matthew 8:26). Sometimes we feel that our faith is little, too. But Jesus said even faith as small as a mustard seed is powerful faith.

Live it! Sometimes we think adults never have problems, but you might be surprised! Talk with the adults in your family about times when you felt you had little faith and let them share their times with you.

Faith When we get angry and lose our temper, life can be pretty miserable. It's important to take time to talk together about what is bothering us or what made us angry. Time is one of the most important gifts you can give to the people in your life.

Live it! Some families have family meetings on a regular basis. Take time together as a family and have a family meeting. This is a good opportunity to talk about problems, check each other's schedules, and plan for upcoming events.

TEN COMMANDMENTS

Faith Many people save mementos or souvenirs after they have been on a trip or to a special event. We may also collect mementos that represent other important aspects of our lives. Our Christian faith is an important part of life. What are some mementos of your faith?

Live it!

Sometimes parents keep small children busy during a church service by having them count things they see, like crosses. Notice the symbols of your faith that you see and count them for a day. Compare lists with each other.

FAITH STORIES

FAITH Why do you think the Ten Commandments were written on stone tablets? Maybe it was because stone was a solid material and the rules couldn't change after they were chiseled in the stone. Why have Ten Commandments at all?

LIVE IT! Do you know the Ten Commandments by heart? The Ten Commandments are an important thing for Christians to memorize. Try rewriting them to be meaningful in your life today. How does your wording change them?

TEN COMMANDMENTS

Faith If you have ever been in a situation where you were afraid or unsure, you probably have prayed to God for comfort or guidance. When was a time that your faith played an important part in your life?

Live it! Ask the oldest living family member to think back to a time when his or her faith was really important to him or her. How was it different to live as a Christian then compared to now?

FAITH The First Commandment says, "You shall have no other gods." What does this mean to you? In what ways is this an important commandment for life today?

LIVE IT! If you had other gods in your life, what would they be? Do you think the other people in your family would have the same gods? How might your gods change as you get older?

16

TEN COMMANDMENTS

FAITH Have you ever read the words in Deuteronomy 11:18-20? These words tell us to remember God's Word. What parts of the Bible have you memorized?

LIVE IT! Have everyone in your family take the name of another family member. Spend time reading in your Bible and find a "promise verse" for that person. Share the verses and then memorize them.

Faith The Third Commandment reminds us to keep the Sabbath, a day of rest, as a holy day. Martin Luther encouraged us to hear and learn God's Word on the Sabbath. In some countries, no stores or businesses are even open on Sundays. How else might we keep the Sabbath?

Live it! Besides going to church, how is Sunday different for you than any other day of the week? How could it be more special?

TEN COMMANDMENTS

FAITH Jesus said whenever we feed the hungry, clothe the poor, help the sick, or visit those in prison, we do the same to him. Read about this in Matthew 25:31-46. Have you done this?

LIVE IT! Put together a family plan to join with others in a worship service at a homeless shelter, nursing home, or other place where you could share God's love with others.

Faith Have you ever played a game called "Gossip" or "Telephone"? It's amazing to see how the beginning message changes by the time it reaches the end of the circle. Do you remember a time someone said something about you that wasn't true? What did you do?

Live it! The Eighth Commandment tells us not to bear false witness against our neighbors, which means, we shouldn't lie about what others have done. With your family members, discuss how the Golden Rule might apply to how we speak about others.

18

TEN COMMANDMENTS

Faith It's been said that even though we may take a vacation, God never takes a vacation from us. In fact, sometimes a vacation is a more relaxed time when we can listen to God more closely than the rest of the year.

45
WORSHIP

Live it! If you take a family vacation, plan your own worship services. Take along a songbook or tape of favorite songs, candles, and a Bible. Have everyone join in planning the service as you worship where you are. As an alternative, visit a church in the area.

Faith In the service of Baptism we are promised that through the waters of Baptism we are reborn children of God and made members of the church, the body of Christ. When is your baptismal birthday? What are some special things you remember about that day?

Live it! Plan a baptismal birthday party for each family member on his or her special day. Light his or her baptismal candle (or another candle) as you pray together for God's continued blessing and guidance.

19
BAPTISM

Faith Have you ever helped during the worship service—singing, serving communion, reading the lessons, or ushering? What made this experience different from just sitting in the pew?

Live it! People of all ages can help with the worship service. Make a gift of your family's time and talents for a worship service, and offer to help in whatever way is needed.

Faith In the service of Baptism, the pastor says that you are sealed by the Holy Spirit and marked with the cross of Christ forever. The pastor makes the sign of the cross on your forehead while saying these words. What does it mean to be marked with the cross of Christ forever?

Live it! Some people think of a cross as just a piece of jewelry. To a Christian, the cross is much more than this. If you don't already have a special cross to wear, buy or make one that will be meaningful to you and remind you that you are marked with Christ's cross forever.

FAITH Some people like traditional worship services. Other people like more contemporary music and words. Which do you like?

LIVE IT! Does your church have more than one kind of worship service? If it does, try going to a different service from the one you normally attend. If not, visit a church that does have different kinds of services.

FAITH What does it mean to be "reborn"? Jesus talked a lot about new life. Are there signs and symbols of new life that remind you of your life as a child of God?

LIVE IT! Buy narcissus or other bulbs of plants that will bloom inside. Fill a pot with dirt, plant the bulbs, and then place a layer of pebbles over them. Water and watch for signs of new life!

21
BAPTISM

Faith Some people say they don't need to go to church because they can worship God anywhere. This is true, but the first disciples knew how important it was to come together to worship God and to encourage and pray for one another. It still is today.

Live it! Make a list of all the parts of your worship service that are a group activity and all the things that can be done by you alone. How does each part help you?

FAITH As Christians, certain symbols are important to us. Water and a seashell are often used as symbols of Baptism. How can symbols be a memory tool for Christians?

LIVE IT! Make your own symbol of your faith. Cover a piece of cross-shaped wood with shells and hang it where you will always be reminded of your new life in Baptism.

22
BAPTISM

Faith "I was glad when they said to me, 'Let us go to the house of the Lord!'" (Psalm 122:1).

Worship is an important part of our lives as the children of God.

Live it! Have you ever gotten up late on a Sunday morning, gone to church in a grumpy mood, and come home feeling like you haven't worshiped at all? Choose one Sunday when everyone in your family gets up an hour earlier, has breakfast together, and then goes to church. Notice the difference.

Faith Your godparents may be an important part of your faith life. They, along with our parents, grandparents, aunts, uncles, and the congregation, promise that they will teach you about living a life of faith. What are some things you know about your godparents? What do they know about you?

Live it! Write a thank-you note or letter to your godparents, thanking them for the part they play in your Christian life. If you don't know them very well, find a way to get to know them better!

23
BAPTISM

FAITH Holy Communion is a time to reflect on God's gifts to you. It is a time to give thanks and praise to God and a time to remember the sacrifice God made for you.

LIVE IT! How does Holy Communion help you live your life? Make the service of Holy Communion more meaningful for your family by volunteering to help the pastor and worship leaders usher and serve communion on one or more Sundays.

Faith A light is an important symbol of a Christian's faith. Jesus said not to keep your light under a basket, but to let it shine for everyone to see. What do Jesus' words mean in your life?

Live it! Have you ever had a meal by candlelight or sat around a campfire and talked? Next time you and your family have a family meeting, do it around a candle or a fire. Talk about how your life can be like that light, shining in the darkness.

Faith The bread and wine are important parts of Holy Communion. The body and blood of Christ come in with and under these two common elements. What communion service has been especially important to you? Why was it special?

Live it! In some churches, families take turns baking the bread to be used for communion. Other families make the wine. See if you can do this at your church, and bring it forward during the service as part of your offering.

Faith The disciples asked Jesus to teach them to pray. Who taught you to pray? When did you learn the Lord's Prayer?

Live it! Have you ever been in church, praying the Lord's Prayer with everyone, and realized that people all over the world and through thousands of years have prayed the same words? Next time you pray this prayer, take time to really think about what you are saying to God.

25
LORD'S PRAYER

Faith The Christian faith is rich with symbols. Close your eyes and think about the service of Holy Communion at your church. What symbols, sights, sounds, and smells come to mind?

Live it! Next time you take Holy Communion, be sure to notice the sights, sounds, and smells that surround the Sacrament of the Altar. Ask the other people in your family if they remember the same things.

26
LORD'S PRAYER

FAITH When we separate the parts of the Lord's Prayer, we find that each petition fits a need we have. Do you ever worry over what you should pray about? Use the Lord's Prayer as your guide.

LIVE IT! Write your own family version of the Lord's Prayer, using the petitions as guidelines. Write up a copy of your family version for each person to use when you have devotions.

FAITH Jesus said, "This cup is the new covenant in my blood." The word *covenant* means "promise." Because of this covenant, you have forgiveness for your sins.

LIVE IT! A covenant is a promise. God made covenants with people in the Bible. Can you think of one covenant God made? (Hint: You can find one in chapter 12 of Genesis!)

Faith The Lord's Prayer has some words that we don't usually use today. *Hallowed* is one of these words—it means "holy." What does the word *holy* mean to you?

Live it! In the book of Exodus, God told Moses to stop and remove his sandals because the ground he was standing on was holy ground. Your life has holy ground in it, too. How do you share your faith with the people who share your holy ground?

27
LORD'S PRAYER

36
COMMUNION

Faith Matthew, Mark, Luke, and Paul write about the night of the Last Supper. The last meal that Jesus shared with the disciples is the meal that Christians share around the world in his memory and to experience his presence. What do you think about when you are communing?

Live it! Read the words used in the service of Holy Communion. Notice that before each portion, Jesus gave thanks. Have you remembered to give thanks today?

Faith The Lord's Prayer refers to the kingdom of God. What do you think God's kingdom is like?

Live it! How would life be different if we lived our lives as if God's kingdom was already here on earth? Try living this way for a day and see if you aren't more grateful, loving, and full of peace.

Faith The first apostles were called to make disciples of all nations and to share the gospel throughout the world. As followers of Christ, what does this mean to you today?

Live it! There are families in many countries who are in need of the basic necessities of life—food, clean water, and shelter. Find an organization your family can support, to help and witness to a family in another country.

Faith The Fourth Petition of the Lord's Prayer says "Give us today our daily bread." As we pray these words, we're asking for more than just physical nourishment. What do you need for your life besides food to eat? Make a list.

Live it! Look at the list you made. What do you need most—what things are most important for us as we live the way God would have us live? Do you know people who don't have these important things? How can you and your family share what you have with those who are without?

LORD'S PRAYER

Faith The Third Article of the Apostles' Creed is about being made holy. Without our own understanding or strength, the Holy Spirit calls us, enlightens us with gifts, and sets us apart for a special purpose. What gifts and purpose do you feel the Holy Spirit has given you?

Live it! Teaching, preaching, caring, sharing . . . all are gifts we can share with the body of Christ in our local church.

What are some of your gifts? Think about ways you and your family can share your gifts with your church in the coming year.

APOSTLES' CREED

FAITH Sin is something many people don't want to talk about. Although we want God to forgive our sins, it can be hard to forgive others. Why is that?

LIVE IT! The Fifth Petition of the Lord's Prayer tells us to forgive others as God forgives us. Forgiving others can be very hard. Who is someone you need to forgive? It's never too late!

30
LORD'S PRAYER

Faith The death and resurrection of Jesus Christ has redeemed you. You are free and you belong to God. How do you use your freedom as a child of God to share the gospel with others?

33

APOSTLES' CREED

Live it! Many people start coming to church because their friends invite them. Have you invited your friends and their families to church lately? Do it this week—they might just be waiting for an invitation.

FAITH There are powerful words in the Apostles' Creed. What do the words *I believe* mean to you?

LIVE IT! How do you show your belief in Christ by the things you say and do every day? Talk about this with the other people in your family and share ideas about how to do this.

31
APOSTLES' CREED

FAITH "I believe in God, the Father almighty, creator of heaven and earth." These words come from the First Article of the Apostles' Creed. What do you like most about God's creation?

LIVE IT! Reread the creation story in the first chapter of Genesis. List the ways you care for God's creation.